M
PEACE
A JOURNEY TO SERENITY

HARSH M. CHHEDA
(HMCKBC)

Made with ♥ on the Notion Press Platform
www.notionpress.com

This book is dedicated to My Param Gurudev.

Adhyatmayogiraj Param Pujya Jainacharya

Shri Kalapurna Suriji Maharaj

Prashantmurti Param Pujya Jainacharya

Shri Tirthbhadra Suriji Maharaj

with all his disciples

and

My MOM

Shri Usha Mayur Chheda

without them, this would have never been possible.

Contents

Contents

Divine Blessings

Param Pujya Acharya Shri Kanak Suriji Maharaja
Param Pujya Acharya Shri Devendra Suriji Maharja
Param Pujya Acharya Shri Kalapurna Suriji Maharaja
Param Pujya Acharya Shri Kalaprabh Suriji Maharaja
Param Pujya Acharya Shri Kalpataru Suriji Maharaja
Param Pujya Acharya Shri Kumudchandra Suriji M. S.
Param Pujya Acharya Shri TirthbhadraSuriji Maharaja
Param Pujya Panyas Shri Tirthrati Vijayji Gani
Param Pujya Panyas Shri Tirthruchi Vijayji Gani

PREFACE

When I look at new generations, there is just a thought that comes to my mind, people are losing their culture. This one thought makes me put my efforts into a younger audience. Problems like stress, anxiety, and depression are increasing throughout the country with rapid westernization. due to this, suicidal attempts among teenagers have also increased. Unfortunately, teenagers and early adults have been deprived of real cream knowledge about themselves. They have never been told about spiritualism, which is the best way to overcome most mental problems.

With God's grace and blessings, I got to know about spiritualism with detailed explanations. With its help, I was able to enter spiritualism and experience the bliss of it. Once I experienced that happiness, I felt like giving this happiness to everyone. This was not an easy task, but my wish to do so was encouraging me all the time. Finally, after many efforts, I have completed this and I am happy to become the youngest spiritual author.

In this book, you will have to think a lot at every point, you will have to analyze yourself and rectify as well. this book will help you attain mental peace and happiness. All you have to do is read properly, understand, and apply. Try to read the whole book at least three times for better understanding. Do share this book with others after reading it, this will help more people to become mindful and self-awaken. This book can also be gifted and read when you feel low.

I hope this book helps you grow spiritually.

- Harsh M. Chheda
2nd July 2020, Mumbai

Acknowledgements

I am thankful to the whole Shri Vimlaben Chandrakant Khetshi Chheda family. Their support and love have always helped me reach new heights of success. I would also like to mention my aunt Shri Deepa Shah and my eldest sister Bansi Shah for guiding and supporting me always. I thank Yashvi, Bhumee, Dev, Devanshi, Vaishvi, Hetvik, Shrey, Vatsal, Kavya, Krisha, Tanisha, and Jaini as well for always being there for me. They have also played a vital role in this book. Mainly Naysha and Shanaya who helped me get the idea of writing this book.

I also express my gratitude towards my Mahek Sir and all the teachers from SVDD School. The base of my building is strong only because of them. I thank all my relatives, friends, Kalyan Mitra, and all the near and dear ones for being a great guide throughout. I would also like to mention my community Shri Vagad Visa Oswal for helping me reach here.

FOREWORD

I have just tried to cover the universal laws and factors in this book. Since these things are universal, it has a huge possibility that you might have read it somewhere else too. But I am sure that you might have never read it in this format with such a logical analysis. I urge everyone to read the whole book in the chapter-wise format. This will help you understand it better. you will get to read certain things that you might have never read before. As you continue reading, the book will get more logical and interesting. so, complete the book gradually and at a slow pace.

All the examples and logics used in this book are just for helping readers understand the concepts. There is no intention to blame, harm, degrade or disrespect any country, culture, religion, caste, gender, community, or person. If you find anything such, please forgive it as a Human error.

I

Self Check

There was something common every year, every month, every week, every day, every hour, and every second till now. You Know what?

We are existing! And among everyone existing, only a few are those who are not just existing but living!

Are we among those few or the rest? Let's have a Self-Check

ॐ

Dalai Lama said

"*We only live, if the purpose of our life is to get happy*"

ॐ

Here we get to know one thing, if we want to seek something, we are on the path of seeking it and still if we aren't getting it, then there are two possibilities. Either our path is incorrect or if the path is correct, we haven't tried to walk on it. There's also a third reason that I will reveal in the middle of the book. For now, major of us belong to the first possibility. I appreciate it if you have already reached happiness. Reached because happiness is a level! It can't be gained easily. We will understand that in a better way ahead. But here's a disclaimer for you. You are going to face a mixture of logic, reality, and philosophy. For understanding this in a better way you will have to keep your mind open to everything, you will have to think a lot, and you will have to do self-check again and again. Gradually you will get the fun of it.

We all are here to grow mentally. The one who grows mentally with time and experience, is said to have the real wisdom. To be clearer, the one who takes wounds as wisdom can only grow. Growth can be done at any age. Similarly, no age can determine mental growth. It is based on your understanding, and capability to learn.

In the same way, maturity isn't based completely on age. Age can be just a small factor, but it is not all. It's not about how many people you meet, how many experiences you have, or how many years you have lived. It is about how many lessons you have learned, and the level of your calmness.

৪৩

Also, there's a fact that there is no end to growth. The more we learn, the calmer we become, and the more we grow. But for that, there is one more factor that is important which is Mental Health. Our Mental health determines a lot of whether we will be able to grow or not.

Sometimes our mental health is bad, but we are unaware of it. This is a major issue for all of us. We don't know whether we are mentally good or bad. There is nothing wrong even if we are mentally ill. We are humans, and this all happening to us is very common. It is wrong when we hide it or we are unaware of it.

So, let us check our mental health.

II

Are We Good Mentally?

If we want to grow internally, we need to check whether we are fit to grow or not. For that, we need to check our mental health. There was a survey, in which people were asked about how many years they want to live. Surprisingly no one wanted to live more than 60 years. When the reason was asked, they said they were already tired of their existing life and won't like living for long as 100 years. This was a heart-breaking survey.

This made me believe that currently, many people are existing in depression. They are living for just passing days, and not for being happy. They are just existing and not living! Even we need to check, are we one of those? Are we depressed? So, let's check ourselves.

If you are depressed, you might get a thought or a feeling of loneliness. Loneliness is a feeling of sadness caused due to a lack of companions, friends, partners, mates, etc. when you need them. You might also get tired of your life and you may not wish to live long.

ॐ

Let us understand, what's depression. Why does it happen? How to get rid of it.

In simple words, depression is a feeling in which you start doubting yourself, and find everyone to be negative, opposing you. You feel like quitting everything, you lose hope in everything, and you start thinking that everyone is selfish and no one cares about you. You feel like you are lacking something and you start losing self-confidence, you don't feel like meeting people, going out of the house, to different places, trips, etc. You don't feel like living your life, you don't get peace anywhere and you find yourself to be the saddest human being on Earth. You lose hope and interest in life. To be honest, these are the common thoughts that come to the mind of most people who feel themselves to be either depressed or lonely.

ॐ

It's not your fault if you are depressed. It's just a feeling in which you get negative thoughts that, are not in your control.

These thoughts start arising as soon as you start thinking just about the sad parts of your life. When you just start thinking about those sad parts, you call them the most depressive parts.

Apart from these, there are many other causes due to which a person faces depression some of them are

- Stress
- Poor Nutrition
- Anxiety
- Isolation
- Lack Of Sleep
- Loss of interest
- Anger
- Ego
- Craving for Unhealthy Food
- Guilt
- Drugs
- Worrying
- Restlessness
- Suicidal thoughts and activities
- Pornography.

These are the major reasons for depression. Sometimes, they can also be the effects of it. Depression normally leads to many other medical issues like Diabetes, Insomnia, Heart diseases, Chronic pain, Diarrhoea, and Constipation, Inflammation.

ॐ

So now, we know that being in Depression is a harmful issue and still common among youngsters.

There are many reactions to situations, that cause depression in a person. We react negatively when something or someone or some situation goes against us.

When everything doesn't go the way it was planned, we get stressed which leads us to overthink, which is the biggest reason for major mental problems and injuries.

It often happens that we start predicting situations; we start overthinking after a certain level of prediction. We overthink all those possibilities that might never happen. These thoughts do not let you sleep and put you more and more under other negative thoughts. These thoughts take away your attention, focus, peace, joy, happiness, etc.

III

Let's Become mentally Stable

For becoming Mentally stable, we need to get rid of all the negative thoughts we face during the depression.

Now, the question is How to get rid of such thoughts and feelings?

ॐ

1. **Meditation.**

Such thoughts can be overcome by meditation. Meditation is the best way to relax one's mind and body. It helps a person to achieve focus and mainly peace. When you attain a specific level of meditation, you feel like you are in heaven. But for attaining that level of meditation, you need to start with the basics of it.

For reaching the height of anything, there is a need to start from the base.

It is a gradual process.

You need to start focusing on yourself, and your daily chores. You need to pay attention to what you do, how you do it, and why you do it. When you have complete focus on the activities you do, unnecessary thoughts won't blow up your mind. When those unnecessary thoughts stop coming up in your mind, your mind is free from unnecessary worries and anxieties, which are major causes of depression.

After this, the next step is, to go inside yourself. Before peeping inside, there is a need of removing all the thoughts from your mind and inner consciousness. For that complete attention to your activities is necessary as the empty brain is the devil's house. Once your brain is completely free of such thoughts, you can proceed toward the next step.

In the next step, you need to just focus on your breaths. When you inhale, when you exhale, how many times have you completed the breathing cycle.

A breathing cycle consists of an inhale and an exhale. You should have a proper focus on it and your mind should not get diverted to other thoughts let it be anything. If it gets diverted, you are not yet ready for it. Establish your focus on your mind and soul. Once you achieve it, start deep meditation on some positive things, pure things, etc.

The soul is the purest form in the Universe. You can literally feel the soul while you meditate, you may feel that you are flying in the sky, and your body parts, muscles, and joints stop paining after that experience. You get healed mentally and physically after this experience.

You lose control over the body while meditating. You feel light-weighted, you just go deep into yourself to meet your soul. While doing this, there has to be complete peace in your mind with no thought in it.

If you are able to do meditation once, it doesn't mean that every time you will succeed in it. Whether you would be able to do it or not, completely gets depended on your mind. There are many types of meditations taught in Indian ancient literature and practices. They are described as 'Dhyan'.

If your mind is empty from all the thoughts, and if you can focus completely on your respiratory cycle, then only you would be able to meditate again in the same way with the same overwhelming experience. You can also focus on something else too. As mentioned above, you can take help of any indian type of meditation. Many have experienced immense joy and peace through this remedy. Also, if you don't want to meditate about yourself, you can meditate about God too.

IV

God, Someone within us

There are many different concepts showing God in a different manner, in different physical forms and persons. But to go simple and universal, Let's not take God as someone but let us take God as virtues. Let us understand God from a completely different angle. Who is God?

God is the purest form of the soul. There are the infinite purest souls or spirits present in the universe. So, with this knowledge, they all are God. A SOUL becomes purest when it has no flaws, defects, demerits, delinquencies, weaknesses, vices, perversions, blemishes, etc. Also, when a soul gets completely detached from all the karmas, Flaws, and Worldly relations, it becomes God. **Even we have the ability to achieve the state of God**. For that, let us understand what are the flaws that we have.

૪૦

18 FLAWS OF A BEING

We have tried to include all the flaws in the major 18 flaws. Let's understand them.

1. Violence
2. Speaking Lies/Half-Truths
3. Stealing anything without the permission of the owner OR Theft
4. Unchastity, Sensual. (It includes Masturbation and sex)
5. Possessiveness. (Keeping more stuff than required is called unnecessary possession, the feeling of attachment towards those possessions is Possessiveness)
6. Anger.
7. Arrogance and Ego. (It includes self-respect, self-esteem, etc everything related to self)
8. Cunningness and Deceit.
9. Greediness. (A feeling that keeps you unsatisfied always)
10. Attachments (Let it be a thing or a person or self)
11. Hatredness and Animosity or Hostility.
12. Quarrelling and Arguing.
13. Making false Accusations or Blaming Others.
14. Gossiping about others.
15. Criticizing anyone or anything.
16. Likes and Dislikes.
17. Deceitful Lying.
18. Having false (wrong/opposite to actual) faiths or beliefs.

૪૦

These all are our flaws, that put us in various and unusual negative states of mind. When we are free from all of them, and we are just occupied with virtues, we attain liberation and we also become God. God is someone who has no flaws, nor any attachment to any of this worldly pleasure or wealth which are all the possessions of relations, Money, Rules, Land, etc. God is enjoying eternal peace, endless happiness, in complete liberation. You can meditate about such God and you will be positive, healed, and in peace.

V

How Does Meditation Help?

Meditation helps in curing many mental and physical problems such as migraine, cancer, anxiety, brain tumor, insomnia, blood pressure, diabetes, etc. The main part of it is that it has no side effects on you. It provides you with tranquillity and physical relaxation. It also increases your focus, and mindfulness, and further helps you heal yourself, as well as others.

ॐ

Meditation is the best way to cure any mental problem gradually, but still, there are chances of it arising again. If we want to stop mental problems from appearing again, we need to understand the base of it and have to remove the base from our life. If you cut the tree without destroying its roots, there are chances that the tree blossoms again. Similarly, if we don't cut the roots of mental problems, we won't get complete liberty from them. So, let's know the roots of psychic issues. Any mental problem starts with stress, irritation, and other issues like irregular sleep, lack of nutritious food, junk food, etc. Majorly the stress, taken by people most of the time, is just overthinking. They worry about their future, their kids, their relations, their elders, and their friends. There are genuine reasons also which keep on giving stress to people such as the death of some near person, some negative news about people or any possessions that someone owns, the pressure of education or wealth. We have understood meditation's effects and we will understand it further in a deeper way but till then let us understand a story, a race behind which there is every one of us.

VI

Human Life, A Race.

There are billions of people we know, who have human life. But everyone follows the same lifestyle, where they keep on repeating the same things, rather than realizing the true facts. Maybe it is important for a cycle to run, but what I mean here is, we don't realize even if our day just passes away, without having something good in it. If we are humans, we have got the power to stay happy, then why can't we? Because we don't know what happiness is. We keep on finding it at the wrong places, then we won't get it for obvious. Let us understand a scene for getting clear on this concept.

In childhood, when someone takes a toy or something similar, away from the child, the child feels to be the saddest person in the house. In teenage life, people have an interest in crushes, attractions, love, etc. When they grow up older, they find interest in Jobs, owning House, Marriage, and kids, after growing more and reaching the age of 40s, they see interest in their children, At the age of 55, Their children marry, and by the age of 60, they become grandparents, and after that, they live a retired life but still, they don't get peace.

At different ages, the same person has different modes and mediums for becoming happy. But the person never gets happy because of greed, dissatisfaction, envy, jealousy, etc. We have many misconceptions in our mind that happiness lies in other things and people and similarly we blame people, situations, and things when we become unhappy for anything. We just blame everyone for sad parts of our lives and similarly, we keep on expecting and demanding things from different people at separate levels.

If life goes against our expectations, we become sad and, if it goes in our favor we think, we have the best life. It is our expectations and demands that make us unhappy and not the situation or the person. When we expect something, we establish an attachment toward that demand. If something opposite to that demand happens, we get a feeling of hatred and it does not let us be at peace. Whenever mental peace is hindered, you have chances to overthink. We don't accept everything the way it is, and we get harassed mentally by ourselves.

Let's understand this in a better and a deep way. But for that we need to ask ourselves, do we really want to get Happy forever? If yes, do we know what Happiness is? To achieve anything, we need to know what it is in detail. We can't just go to the market and say I want something but I don't know how it looks, what it is in real or what it is called. We can be fooled by the product if we are unaware of the reality. The same is with happiness. To understand it, Let us dive deep into it.

VII

Happiness, just a normal feeling?

Just ask yourself, **WHAT IS HAPPINESS?**

Happiness is a feeling, behind which everyone is running, and which is always hidden from those who don't even know what it is. It is there with only those, who know what it is in true form. To be serious, you need to know about something you want. Without even knowing what you want, you will never get it. Most of us don't know what happiness is, and hence we are not getting it. Happiness is a feeling that everyone wants all the time. No one ever gets bored of it, even if given in excess. So, let's take the definition of it as

"*Happiness to be A Feeling from Which, We Never Get Bored.*"

Whenever someone asks us, what is happiness according to us, we start giving answers that by doing this or that, we get happy. We are never clear about this concept. Now take your answers and our definition of Happiness into consideration, and just try to match them. You will realize that they both go parallel, they never meet each other. It means that your beliefs about happiness are wrong. By doing anything or by achieving anyone or anything, you don't get happiness. It is just like an illusion of actuality but not reality. Illusions often lead to misunderstandings and a feeling of hatred in the later part. It is a bit confusing to understand right now, so to make it easier to understand, let us take a few examples.

Let us take a food item.

Suppose a person says that a cold drink gives happiness. When a person sitting in an air-conditioned room for a whole day is given a glass of a cold drink, he will find it to be good, whereas a person who did physical work in a temperate climate, is given the same glass of a cold drink, he feels like he got heaven. It is the same Cold drink, the same quantity, just two different people with two different situations, and the level of satisfaction varies to a great extent. Similarly, if the same 8-9 glasses of Cold drink are given to the same two people, the last few glasses of the same drink would become painful as their stomachs would get full.

Let us take one more example for a better understanding.

Suppose a person is starving for 8 to 9 hours. The person is a foodie and gets happy when gets to eat pizza ordinarily. After staying hungry for 8 to 9 hours, when that same person is given his beloved Pizzas from which he gets happiness normally, will put that person under a different level of joy. The first pizza will be eaten with great joy and enjoyment, gradually his hunger will vanish and he will be full. Now if he is asked to eat more such as two pizzas, he will feel like vomiting. He would be uneasy!

In the first example, one person was more thirsty, tired, had physical pain, and hence got more satisfaction from the cold drink. The other person was just resting and so the other person was not that thirsty and hence another person was not satisfied with the cold drink as much as the first person. In the second example, a person was hungry for many hours and then he got his favorite food which was pizza. After eating one or two pizzas that person got satisfied, but after having his stomach full, he felt uneasy and he couldn't eat the same pizza that satisfied him a few minutes ago.

[**Note:** - In the explanation of the above two examples, the words 'satisfied' and 'satisfaction' are used. Here, they are used for denoting happiness. A person can never be satisfied with the food that is eaten only once because the body needs it for functioning every day.]

In both the above examples, we saw that if the person has faced some problem/situation (thirst and fatigue for the first one, hunger for the second example), then only he gets happiness, similarly when these thirst/fatigue/hunger, etc. go away, even the happiness you were experiencing vanishes away. It means that till there is any kind of suffering, you can get happiness, once those sufferings end, those modes of happiness become the reason for new sufferings. We can conclude that the absence of suffering is happiness according to us. Till there is suffering, some relief from it seems to be happiness, but in actuality, it is just an illusion. So, the happiness we are experiencing, is not happiness in real life! but it is just an absence of suffering or relief to a certain type and certain level of pain.

VIII

Understanding Happiness in a better Way.

To go deeper into this topic, we need to understand certain facts that we never even think of. We never understand that in the materials, you are just forgetting your pain or suffering from some situation or thing or person for just some time. In simple words, you are just getting distracted from the painful things or your dislikes. While getting distracted, you are away from your problems or dislikes which keep you happy for a few minutes or hours, or days. Let us take one more example for understanding this concept.

Suppose a person has to go to his workplace walking every day, which is somewhere painful for him. When he thinks of it, he wishes for a cycle. When he gets a cycle, he is satisfied and he is happy. After 6 months, he changed his job and now he has to travel by train for reaching his workplace. Now he has no use of his cycle and he has to maintain it, which is not affordable for that person. Now that person thinks that it would be better if he never bought that cycle. Till there was the pain of walking, the cycle gave him satisfaction, when there was no pain of walking, the same cycle no longer satisfied him or made him happy but instead gave him unhappiness.

Similarly, in life when you use old things, you don't like using those old things, which means they don't make you happy, but you have no option at certain times. When you get a good exchange of the same thing, you think that you are happy. But when this new exchange becomes old, you don't like using it also. This cycle keeps on repeating for things and even people.

So now we know that nothing can give you happiness. now let us take this to people. we understood that after a point we will get bored of the same thing and happiness means that it's a feeling from which we never get bored. So, happiness is not present in any of the things, because we get bored of things very easily and very soon.

Let's talk about people.

Many say that they get happiness while talking to someone, or spending time with someone, etc. So, let's clear our concept first.

"We Find Happiness Outside Because We are Not Getting It In Our Self."

When we get bored with our daily life, we just try to open up ourselves in front of someone we like. We share our things, our plans, and our feelings with that person. We like it when the person listens to us, understands us, gives us positive reactions, etc. But after time, the same person seems to be changed. Most of the time, it's not the person who changes, it is just our mindset that never gets satisfied and needs variety.

It's agreed that sometimes even people change. They don't remain in the same way as they were before. But we can't accept the fact that the person has changed. We just can't accept such facts because we had expected many things and all our expectations broke down.

It is our flaw that we expect. Expectations can be the biggest reason for most mental problems. Even our body does not listen to us. We cannot control organs or any other part of our body. If we expect our body to stay healthy always, if we expect our body to stay fit always, if we expect our body to stay beautiful always, it is our foolishness, that we expect something opposite to its nature.

Similarly, we expect thousands of things from people, things, and situations. When something goes opposite to our expectations, we go under deep thoughts, stress, and sometimes depression. So earlier, we understood Depression in a basic manner. But gradually we will think with deeper perspectives.

Each and every person has a space and a boundary. That he expects no one to cross.

IX

Can we get rid of Depression easily?

Before taking any medicine for any illness, we need to know the reason for it, just in a similar way, for getting rest from Depression we need to understand the cause of it in a detailed manner.

we expect thousands of things from people, things, and situations. When something goes opposite to our expectations, we go under deep thoughts, stress, and sometimes depression.

> *"Depression comes because most of the time, we don't accept reality."*

When our body does not listen to us and work according to us, how can we expect someone to listen to us always and work according to us?

No one will remain the same, no one will stay forever. Change is a universal rule to which there is no option for anyone to escape.

Learn to Accept, Leave to Expect, and life shall become easier than ever.

So, if we think that spending time with someone gives us happiness, then this is also a misconception. Because you can never spend your full time with the same person even for some days, then without getting bored, spending your whole life with the same person is impossible. Happiness is a feeling from which you never get bored. It comes with such activities which will never make you bored of them, even if u do them your whole life. Spending time with the same person will make you bored of it, after a particular time so telling that it gives you happiness is a misconception. It may give you joy, but it surely does not give you Happiness.

> "*If we learn to accept it, it won't give us much mental pain and imbalance.*"

When you have nothing to do, you are alone, and you feel lonely and sad. These feelings give you unhappiness, but when you get someone's company after a long time, you feel like it gives you happiness but it's just a distraction from the feeling of unhappiness given by loneliness. Once you feel that, you have nothing more to talk about, you have no topic to talk about, and you feel bored with the same person you thought, spending time is giving you happiness, but it is just an illusion as we understood it earlier.

We can apply the rule of Economics, and understand this concept with more clarity. Economics teaches us that if the Supply Increases, Demand decreases, and if the Supply Decreases or gets stopped, Demand rises suddenly.

When you have everyone to talk to, you don't give them much value or you can say that you don't understand their true value. Similarly, when you have no one to talk to, you feel the true value of companions. So, when you have no one to talk to, you feel sad, lonely, and unhappy but when you get someone to talk to, you get rid of your loneliness and sadness. Getting rid of it seems to be happiness which is an illusion. Later on, when you have been talking with the same person for many days and months, you feel bored with that same person, who used to give you happiness at a point. You can never get happy with the same person or a thing until you get satisfied. But we never get satisfied, instead, we get bored and we want variety everywhere.

There is a possibility that you get satisfied with one person only throughout your life. In that case, you will be at peace and happiness. This peace will be ultimate but it won't be the product of a person's love and care but it will be the result of your satisfaction.

So, when we expect something from someone or something, it is not necessary that our expectations will be fulfilled. When they don't meet your expectations, there is a need for you to accept them, or else you will get sad which develops into depression gradually. Acceptance is necessary without it; you can never achieve Mental Peace.

Whenever we don't accept situations, things, or reality, we get upset with reality, and we get sad, that is because the reality is something different than what we expected. We don't get sad sometimes, but most of the time we are not able to accept the sad truths or realities of our life. If you are depressed, you need to first bring acceptance to yourself. At the roots of depression, there lies rejection (which is a lack of acceptance), and many more expectations.

X

Depression and its roots.

ॐ

Roots are the starting or initial stage of any plant. So, if we cut the roots, the tree would not grow again, similarly, if we bring acceptance in us, depression can't grow from its roots. Depressive thoughts are building and its base or the initial stage is negative thoughts coming up, due to not fulfilling your expectations. Sometimes we go into negative thoughts because of overthinking about the future. This overthinking leads us to stress, anxiety, and most probably negative expectations. This might be confusing to understand, so let us take a few examples on this topic.

ॐ

There was a housewife. She was watching a television serial and in that, she saw, the husband in the serial brings many gifts for his wife without reason for just making his wife happy. Now the housewife got influenced by this serial and developed the thought that her husband does nothing to make her happy. She started expecting many things from her husband and she started recollecting all the wrong things her husband did to her or all flaws her husband has. She started expecting so much, which was beyond the limits of her husband. She started comparing every other husband with her husband.

For bringing some happy parts in her life from her husband, she started thinking so much which took her to the path of so much stress, that she got diabetes. Her husband couldn't meet all of her expectations and she used to get frustrated every time her husband didn't complete her expectation. In every small thing, she started finding a mistake in her husband. She forgot what happiness was.

No doubt that her husband might also be wrong at some point but because of her nature of expecting a lot, she never got happy. She always was sad about what she didn't get and not happy about what she got. She started doubting her earlier decisions, her husband, and herself. But in the end, she got sad because she couldn't find anything. Everything was the same, except for her perspective.

Earlier, she was positive about everything. She was happy about all the small things her husband did for her. But then a serial changed her perspective and she became sad for the rest of her life. If she would have accepted her husband the way he was, she would be experiencing happiness, but instead, she counted all his flaws and started blaming him instead of accepting him and as a result, she became sad.

ॐ

Here we can understand to what extent expectations can destroy us.

> ## "EXPECTATIONS WILL BURN YOU FIRST AND THEN ANY OTHER PERSON AROUND YOU."

We took a housewife, and serial in the above example but the same story can be taken with any other person irrespective of gender, age, and income status. Also, Television serials can be replaced by any friend/friends, any social media posts, any other couples, etc. The same story can happen to anyone, at any place, and at any time.

Let us take another few examples.

There was another woman. She had married a person living in a joint family. She had her mother-in-law, father-in-law, and brother-in-law staying with her husband. They were too negative by nature. This woman used to give her 100% in her work but still, her in-laws removed faults from it. Her in-laws used to remove mistakes in almost everything she did. They used to trouble her and torture her mentally. Also, they never gave her privacy, they never trusted her for any small thing also. But still, she always thought that there were some mistakes in herself. she started improving herself from the mistakes her family members removed. She still gave her best for the family, she gave them love even if she was getting hatred from them. She continued to keep her Goodness intact. And magic happened. Gradually changes were seen in her family. Her in-laws started trusting her. They started giving her privacy, they started praising her, and they started giving her love. She won a place of dignity and respect in her family. This all was the outcome of her positivity and patience. She could have become depressed, she could have become negative, she could have lost her temper, and she could have done every such thing that could hinder her happiness and joy of living life. But because she stayed positive and since she kept enough patience, life started showing up positive results.

ॐ

Here again, we understand that our thoughts and mindset act as a magnet for all the types of things we are facing or are coming across. So, we can conclude that,

ॐ

"We attract things and people according to our thoughts."

ॐ

XI

Let's learn meditation in detail.

In life, we can either be negative or positive. There can't be both. Unstable thoughts between negative and positive are also considered to be negative only. Negative thoughts normally obstruct your joy, it makes you think about the negative things going around you in life and after that, you are not able to focus on the work you do, and you are not able to live joyfully. You just face negative thoughts; you just overthink a lot. You might feel very relatable to this, but to be honest, this is a common situation with every person around and there's nothing to worry about. Due to overthinking, you just get into a vibe where you don't want to talk to anyone, you don't want to communicate with anyone. You feel bored, you feel left out too sometimes. For some, this might help them to heal, but for some, this might even become worse. If you want to avoid everything like that, the best way you have is, to be happy with yourself. For that again, we have a therapy called **MEDITATION**.

ॐ

So, let us continue the topic. Previously we understood, the advantages of meditation. But now, let us understand this topic in more detail. Meditation is something that makes you feel your soul. The soul is the purest form of virtues, energy, knowledge, and happiness. The soul is the most self-sufficient thing on the planet. The only destination of infinite knowledge, infinite energy, infinite happiness. So, meditation is the process wherein the initial stage you meet your soul, after some progress, you start feeling your soul, and after becoming perfect, you start living your soul. Living your soul means, you need to go within, you need to feel the inner you, the actual you. While feeling yourself, you won't even know what is happening with your body. The topic that has started is quite deep now, and at the same time tough to understand and believe. But trust me, this is something you won't believe unless you feel it yourself.

ॐ

The soul is an immortal being that is full of virtues, values, and goodness. It does not have fear of any being or thing, it does not have hatred for any creature, what it has is just a thought that Everyone gets eternal peace and happiness as soon as possible. At the same time, the soul enjoys itself always, it does not wish for anything or a person to make it happy. It just enjoys its own company and since it has no wishes or expectations, no one or thing can take away its peace. Meditation helps in attaining inner peace. The person who attains it gets satisfied within the self and becomes self-sufficient for their happiness.

For attaining such an amazing level of peace and happiness, we need to meditate. At the start, we can meditate by just diverting our attention to our respiration. This will support establishing focus and getting rid of thoughts. When you start meditating you might not be able to control your thoughts but gradually you will learn it. Once you succeed in attaining focus and once you get control over thoughts, you need to start loosing up your body. You need to leave your body loose. Gradually, you will realize that you have lost control over your body, and you will feel like you are so light-weighed that you are flying in the air. It's hard to believe and much harder to reach that level but it is not impossible. You can do it too!

There are some more tips, that will help you increase your focus while meditating. In actuality, those aren't tips but necessities for meditation, but their implementation takes many efforts, and hence you can just give it a try.

XII

Senses and their Likes & Dislikes

ॐ

If you want to meditate well, what you have to do is you need to first get control over all your senses. There are five senses and each sense has some likes and dislikes. Based on those likes and dislikes, our attitude keeps on deviating. The senses aren't only 5 organs but they are a form of life in the body. They help in knowing things. But the problem comes when it comes to likes and dislikes. Knowing the nature of a thing in the terms of feel, taste, smell, observation, and sound is good till it is useful for just knowing, but once we start liking something and hating something, it comes to our peace. Senses make us know our likes and dislikes. But we can also say that senses only have likes and dislikes for any object or thing. There are five senses and a ruler sixth sense and each sense has some likes and dislikes. Based on those likes and dislikes, our attitude keeps on deviating. Let us understand the senses and take a few examples to clarify this concept.

ॐ

The first sense is Skin. It likes feeling soft surfaces, smooth things, and the touch of the opposite gender, and at the same time, it does not like feeling rough, pointed, or sharp things. Now the question arises how does it affect our mental peace? so it's quite simple. You went somewhere and your slippers have broken the way you cannot use them, there's no other shop to buy anything and the road you were walking on, is full of tiny rocks that don't feel good. Now your peace may not sustain due to rocks coming on the way that are pinching you. still, for once you may blame the situation and try to stay in peace. But if someone purposely did this to your footwear, you might become angry and lose your temper and peace. That's because your skin doesn't like it. Because of someone or something, your skin had to face some problems that made you angry. So, the skin's wish to get everything as per its like did not get fulfilled resulting in your mind losing its peace. Let us move forward toward your second sense.

ॐ

Then comes your second sense which is the Tongue. It likes all the good tastes available. if you have a stomach that never fills, your tongue will never stop asking for anything. majorly it is not your body that needs food, but your tongue that needs the taste. similarly, your tongue doesn't like the bitter taste. Just imagine, you have ordered a farmhouse pizza including many veggies from a pizza shop. And they sent you the pizza as per your order, but they just modified it by themselves by adding a bitter guard to it. You haven't eaten the pizza yet and still don't know that it has a bitter guard in it. You ate the first slice and it was so bitter that you couldn't eat the rest of the pizza. You got angry at the seventh sky. You complained to the manager about all this. But nothing could change your destiny of bitter guard. But what we do is blame someone or the other for losing our peace. But in reality, it is the likes and dislikes of our tongue responsible for losing our mental peace. If we would be okay with whatever taste it would have, it could never take our mental peace. Let us move towards our next sense.

༄

The third sense is the Nose. It Likes all the good odors and smells and similarly dislikes all the bad odors and smells. Here good and bad odor is also determined again based on our likes and dislikes. What we like is good, and what we dislike is bad, irrespective of how good work it might be doing. Again, over here, let's take an example. You are in a car with your family. The air-conditioner is on, the car freshener is been sprayed and there is a really good smell in the car. But suddenly, one of the passengers farts and it smelled so bad that everyone started coughing and you lost your mental peace again. Again, if we concentrate, it is not the smell taking away your mental peace, but the dislike of bad smells and wish of having a good smell around you. This concept can still be unclear but I'm sure, you will be clear as we move forward.

༄

The fourth sense is our Eyes. They like seeing cool colors, natural environments, natural beauty, and much more. At the same time, they don't like being around Certain things that hurt them, like smoke coming from the fire, which burns their eyes. Being in front of the screen for a too long time also gives a sensation of burning in your eyes. Again, an example over here. You are going on a road trip in the forest. In the start, your eyes are loving to see everything coming across, but suddenly you saw some grasses and trees burning ahead and the smoke of that fire was causing itching and irritation in the eyes and it burnt them at the same time. Your eyes start watering and again your mental peace does not sustain. Here again, when your eyes disliked the sensation, it caused the loss of your peace. It might be a bit unclear so let us take another example. You are working on your laptop for 10 hours continuously, and now it's hard for your eyes to look at the screen. But unexpectedly, your boss gives you more work of two hours. Your eyes like rest and don't like to get more stressed but since it was an order, you had to do it. Somehow you managed to do work for an hour, but now your eyes, have started burning and watering, and the vision is getting blurred gradually. Now- Again there will be a loss of peace. It's because there is somewhere pain suffered by your eyes. Again, if you aren't able to understand, just move forward and keep reading.

ఴ

The Fifth sense is your Ears. They like melodious music, and songs and they dislike very loud noise, volume, and bass that irritate them. If they hear good songs, at the proper volume, they will surely like them, but if they hear something like ultrasound waves, they won't like it resulting again in the same thing i.e., loss of mental peace. Here I think there is no need for an example as it is easy and clear to understand. But still, if you couldn't understand any of the above five points about the five senses, there is the next sense to explain them all. Yes, there is a sixth sense as well. Let us study about it.

ॐ

The Sixth sense is the Mind. Here I'm not using the term Brain, but I'm stating it as mind as it has a huge meaning difference. In simple language, the brain is a human organ whereas, the Mind is the thinking capacity of any human. It is the sixth sense that drives all five senses. Likes and Dislikes are usually determined by our mind and, according to its determined criteria, all other senses work. So, if you want to achieve mental peace, You need to get control over your mind as it controls all other senses. The mind can also be termed as consciousness. If you are successful in achieving control over your Mind, Thoughts, Likes, and Dislikes no one or nothing can take away your mental peace. Because then it won't be your mind, but you who will be the Driving Force.

Lord Shri Vardhaman Mahaveer Said,

"*Conquering Yourself is better and much more difficult than conquering Millions of enemies. That is the eternal happiness itself.*"

ॐ

Again, a doubt arises, are we separate from our Body?
If Yes, who are we?

We are the powerhouse of the Purest form of energy, power, knowledge, and virtues and in simple words, we are souls. We are separate entities. The body is just a physical and temporary house to this entity. Meditation also helps to feel your real existence i.e., your Soul. It cannot be proven in labs but can be felt after achieving a certain level of meditation. Controlling our thoughts, minds, likes, and dislikes is simply controlling our wishes. As much you wish, the much your wishes and expectations break and it is surely going to take away your mental peace and stability. Today, the world is following westernization, where they believe in living life to the fullest, enjoying, and doing everything that makes you happy for time being. If we talk about staying within ourselves, they will laugh at us the way people laughed at Thomas Edison when he said about light. Going within gives you happiness and peace that can't be taken away at any cost. It is new for those who never felt it, but if you are interested, you must try it. Meditation is the process of going within, being with the real and inner us, who always stays with us, and is always happy.

XIII

The Desires

As we saw in the previous chapter, senses have their likes and dislikes. These likes and dislikes form desires. These desires lead us ultimately towards unhappiness, restlessness, and sorrow. Maybe these desires and wishes don't seem as sorrowful to us, maybe these likes and dislikes don't seem as sorrowful to us. But sometimes, it is not necessary that our belief is correct. We can be wrong too.

ॐ

This is just like alcohol, cigarettes, etc. Most people consuming it, don't find anything wrong with it. But its effects on the human body are proven. They are the type of poison that people take happily. In reality, it's not people drinking alcohol, it is the alcohol that is drinking people and similarly with smoking.

ॐ

A drop of poison may feel similar to water, but you can only distinguish it if you are awakened. Other than that, we feel happiness in all such things mentioned above, only because we haven't experienced real happiness yet.

The one who has never seen sugar, won't understand it ever. You can't explain to a person what sugar is without letting him see it and taste it. And till a person sees and tastes sugar, he will be ready to even believe that salt is only sugar or similar. The reason is, he has never experienced real sugar. Similarly, we have not experienced real happiness and so we feel, that our desires, wishes, and likes make us happy. But again, this is an illusion.

Happiness can only be felt and not expressed. It is the best experience of all. But, it can't be bought or taken from somewhere or something. We can't get it from someone either. We have to achieve it by ourselves. Since we will achieve it from within, it will never go away, as the things coming from outside don't last long. So let us achieve this permanent solution.

Let us move toward reality.

XIV

The Reality

'In this life, everyone is urging Happiness. Let it be humans, animals, insects, or any other being. Everyone wants to live; everyone wants to be happy. No one is wishing to die or be stressed, depressed, or sad either. knowing this fact, we need to understand that everyone deserves happiness. At the same time, each and every being has virtues and many good qualities stored in them. When we start looking at those good qualities and things, we get an optimistic vision toward life and the people around us. This leads to a positive outcome. This outcome itself helps us to develop a positive attitude toward life.

There's a sentence in Sanskrit

'परस्परोपग्रहो जीवानाम्'

It just says that each and every other being. From this, we can just derive that each and every being is helpful to me in some or the other way and I am helping every other being in some or the other way. This helpfulness can be direct or indirect manner as well but it is present. This helps us to know that each and every being is interconnected to each other.

Hence, we should not become selfish and be helpful to each being around us as even they are helpful to us. We need to just be grateful for what we have got. As we become grateful for everything we have, the satisfaction level in life increases by itself. This helps a being to be more kind, calm, and happy. Being will be happy within; being will be confident within.

ॐ

> "When we have something within us, we never seek it from the outside."

For understanding a better way, whenever we produce goods on our own, we won't import them. Once we have those goods in abundance, we start exporting them instead.

Similarly, whenever we have peace from within, whenever we have confidence within, no one in the world has the power to take it away from us as we own it. In the same manner, we won't need it from someone else either.

> "When one is complete within the self, he doesn't bother others and vice versa."

But if we are bothered by someone, or we are bothering someone, it just indicates that we haven't found ourselves.

> "The one who knows self, won't go to find out anything else."

Shri Vardhaman Mahaveer said,

"*The One who found himself has found the whole world and life.*"

The whole world recites within us. Once we find ourselves, we will be able to feel ourselves in each and every living being. We will find each and every second to be beautiful, each and every moment to be best, and each and every life to be good. We will find the new us, who forgot to be sad.

Maybe this sounds lethargic, but trust me! Once you reach that level or once you find yourself, you will be the happiest person. You will experience it all.

This is a reality, maybe very hard to digest or believe, but that's the best part of it.

There is also another sad part of reality.

We humans, start our journey with birth. We study for our living, grow up set up our family, earn for them, buy/ rent a house for them, run behind different objects at a different age, die and here our journey ends.

Animals start their journey with their birth, they observe everything for their livelihood, grow up and set up their family, search for things for survival, make a house somewhere at a good place, run behind different objects at a different age, die and here their journey ends too.

Here we find a few similarities and differences in the lifestyle of humans when compared to animals.

Let us talk about the similarities first.

1. Both of them live in the same style.
2. Both of them protect their family and their possessions. For which they even fight with their own community/ type.

ఞ

Let us talk about differences now.

1. Animals don't harm others for their personal interest, unlike humans. (Necessity is a different case)
2. Animals stay loyal to their owners and partners whereas the current new generation of humans doesn't.
3. Animals live their life according to their nature whereas humans go against nature and even destroy it.
4. Humans have the power to think well, do something good for themselves as well as others, live a healthy lifestyle and do something extraordinary than animals.

The nature mentioned in the second point of differences above, also has some characteristics that let us see them as well.

1. An herbivorous animal will never eat anything beyond plants. **Studies say that the human body is similar to herbivorous.** When scientific comparison was made between herbivorous and carnivorous, we found that human body is more similar to herbivorous animals. But still, humans consume non-veg for taste and for the myth, that it contains more nutrients which we don't get through vegetarian cuisine. All the animals they

consume are vegetarian by nature. So, from where do they get such nutrients?

2. Animals stop eating when they fall ill. Humans do not stop consumption of anything instead they increase sometimes. In ancient India, fasting had a significant role. Our ancestors used to fast before taking any medicine for any illness. Fast of minimum three days was considered to be a body healing therapy. Just doing fast would cure us from any disease. This therapy has now started becoming global, but has been derived from India.

3. Animals avoid eating after sunset and before sunrise whereas humans do exactly the opposite to it.

So, if we compare, animals and humans live almost in the same style! but animals follow their nature. Whereas humans do not follow their nature most of the time but do something opposite to it. We can now conclude that the lifestyle of animals might be better.

Are humans meant to live like animals?
Dr APJ Abdul Kalam said,

"Most people, they raise a family, earn a living, and then they die. Never follow them."

Aren't those words for us? Aren't we doing the same?

Just living like everyone else, makes no difference and gives no value to our life. This is exactly where we stand beside animals. We need to focus more on life, we need to search for the right, a and move towards the reality.

৪৩

XV

The Literacy

The literacy rate around the world is increasing. It is an undenied good factor. But is literacy enough?

People getting literate is undoubtedly a good thing but getting educated is much more important.

Being literate and educated has a difference. Being literate means you have learned about something, you have known something and you know to read and write. But being educated means to understand something, to know everything in basics, to be clear with all the concepts of life and everything around us. Literacy can help you with your existence but your reason for existence can only be known with the help of education.

A literate person will just know things, but his knowledge won't imply much in real life. Most of the unnecessary pollution is caused by literate people. Most of the literate people in India are found throwing waste openly on roads and not in bins. Most literate people are found playing music at high volumes. Most of those literate people are found smoking and praising it too which causes air pollution. Most literate people are found buying things that are not needed. Buying anything without need creates an imbalance between that product and resources. Most of the food and water wastage is done by the same literate people. There's no use of that literacy if you don't understand those basic things which are good and bad for the environment and nation.

Now the question arises who's the educated person?
For that we have another Sanskrit text
खणम् जाणाई पंडिए !

It means that the one who has understood the knowledge after getting it and knows to make wise use of it in life is an educated person. In simple form, the one who knows time is the one who is educated.

What does knowing time mean?

Knowing time means understanding the importance of time. To make the best possible use of time. Not to waste even a single minute on unnecessary stuff. Every minute and second should be spent wisely.

This birth, this year, this month, this week, this day, this hour, this minute, this second, this life! everything is a blessing! Every new day is a new start toward success. Hence each and every second should be of optimum use.

Shri Vardhaman Mahaveer used to always tell his disciple Shri Gautam swami that, don't even waste a single part of a second.

೫

Other than that, we have faced covid era. We have seen people dying, losing their life unexpectedly. People were crying for their admissions to hospitals, for the medicines, food, living and what not. Even after spending crores, not everyone could save the life of their loved ones. Let it be anyone, no one can ever buy time with money.

Therefore, we should understand and make wise use of our time. We have only received a maximum of 100 years, so let's live the best 100 years of all.

೫

Let's live in such a way that your one life becomes enough to be the epitome of Life itself.

೫

What do we need to do to be wise with time?

Here we again have a Sanskrit text.

उपयोगो लक्षणाम्

This means being awakened, conscious, or attentive all the time. This is a trait and characteristic of oneself. Other than that, being awakened completely (enlighten/liberated from the world) is our final goal, for which being awakened is necessary.

We need to be awakened all the time, we need to know each and every second. We need to know what we are doing and why are we doing it. Whatever we did, was it necessary to be done? Have we completed the things that were necessary?

Knowing answer to every question and then making use of time will be really wise. And paying attention to each and every activity will help you focus more, and get peace soon.

&

But for that, you need to inspect yourself with everything.

Being awakened doesn't mean just being conscience about your activity, but it also means being conscience of your own thoughts.

We should know when we get angry, when we come under ego, when we fall for objects, and when we come under our five senses. We don't have to be a slave to our bodies! These things will happen, we need to introspect about them and know them at least. There is nothing wrong with such thoughts and anger. It happens with all. But if we think that having anger and ego is a good thing, then maybe we are making a mistake. We have already discussed this topic in the above chapters, and therefore, I am not taking it in detail here.

But we should know whenever and whatever we are doing. With time we will get awakened and our anger will be easily controlled. For that, we need to recognize it, when it comes.

Only if we understand these all things, we can call ourself as educated. Self-assessment is required at every stage of life for this.

Repeating again, we need to get awakened!
This is the most crucial part of getting peace.

We need to also give more attention to the use of our time. The highest wastage of time is letting our mind get engrossed and diverted in the remaining five senses.

These five senses distract us and mislead us from our goal.

This is the biggest thing that a human can only do and animals can't. By doing this, we are doing something better and different than others. When the whole world will be busy with the slavery of the five senses, you will be enjoying liberation from them.

Slavery because you can't even ignore your senses. They rule on you and give you a lot of internal pain which can be just felt if you are awakened enough.

XVI

Wishes

Our life is filled with wishes. There is no end to wishes of any kind.

Lord Mahaveer Said,

"Wishes are just never-ending Like Sky"

We can feel those words in our daily life. Just like the sky, our wishes too have no starting or ending point. After every minute our wish for anything can either change or can either increase. We, our self don't know what wishes are we going to make in the next 5 minutes. These wishes are connected to our five senses and thus they do not have any ending or satisfying point. They are just going to remain forever.

છ

There is an ideology that, we should complete our wishes as they keep on diverting our attention towards them till we don't complete them. They take away our focus and satisfaction. This ideology isn't correct. The wishes won't end or get satisfied ever. So, if we complete them once, they will rise again in another bigger form.

Let us have an example for more clarity.
I like pasta and I am tempted to eat them today. Something good happened and I got to eat pasta. Now, after having them I liked them so much but I got full. I got satisfied for a few days but again after a few days, I will get temptations for pasta or any other food item. Here the temptations I get are never-ending wishes and a type of joylessness. But as I complete the wish, I feel joy. The joy I felt wasn't because I ate it, but it is because of getting liberation from temptation or wish. This is just like happiness. Again, this is an illusion. In a desert, there is an illusion of water. You feel happy when you see the water, but you never get satisfied as no water is present in real. Similarly completing wishes seems to be joyful but since there is no real happiness in it, we never get satisfied.

"Happiness is not subjected to the body, but to the soul and mind."

XVII

The Spiritual Age

There are many people showing their concerns about the age of a being for practicing Spiritualism. For this, we need to understand that spirituality is not only an ongoing life part but also a life path at the same time. Spiritualism is a healthy practice that should be a part of daily life.

Till a being is practicing it, he is protected from all the outer hardships. Spiritualism doesn't mean leaving everything aside and becoming a monk. Spiritualism is a way of keeping one's self-satisfied and happy. Spiritualism is a way of being your real self and not your body.

Therefore there is no age for practicing it. But we can assure you that it is better to start it from an earlier age.

Spiritualism demands a good body and physical well-being as well. For that purpose, it is better to practice it from small age itself. Once our body starts getting different health issues, we are unable to practice it. Instead, if we start at an earlier age. our body gets saved from many health issues as well.

ॐ

Jainacharya Shri Ratnasundar Suriji said,

""Spiritualism can be practiced at its best in the age of make-up. We cant practice it properly in the age of check-ups.""

Very few words, but of great significance. We can easily understand how crucial the age factor might be for this. So, it is better to practice it at an earlier age.

XVIII

The Discipline

For doing anything great in life, we need to have discipline in our life too. If we go through the life of popular personalities like our beloved **PM Narendra Modi, Actor Akshay Kumar**, etc. we can find a common factor and that is discipline.

They never compromise with their principles in their routine life. This attitude makes them better at their skills. Let it be monks or army officers, everyone has to be at a certain level of discipline and that is the way they are better than anyone else. There are other factors too but discipline plays a vital role in them.

For attaining peace or joy in life, there is a need for self-implied discipline.

Sometimes discipline comes in the form of restrictions. It can be put by parents, teachers, bosses, or even themselves. Most of the time I have seen youngsters hating those restrictions. They feel that their parents don't understand them. To be honest, it is not like that. No one can understand us better than our parents. They know what is good and bad for us.

Therefore, the restrictions bestowed upon us, aren't for just restricting us or keeping us away socially. They are a part of our protection. A car has a break in it but that is not for restricting the speed it is for protecting us from accidents! Similar to speed breakers, seat belts, and traffic signals. These are part of protecting our life. Similarly, discipline levied by parents is a part of protection and not restriction. So we should understand their concern and obey them.

XIX

The Destiny

Not all of our wishes get fulfilled. Some things may become true whereas some don't. This is the reality of life. There is nothing to stress about in this reality. Similarly, we sometimes cry about our situations and blame some other thing or living being for it. To be honest, we just blame when we can't accept reality. This is the complex that we need to understand. Everything happening to us or in our lives is completely based on our past deeds and our destiny. Everyone and everything is just playing a role in our life to help us reach our destiny. No one is responsible for anything. It is you who is responsible for everything in your life. Hence, no one should be blamed.

ॐ

Still, if you feel sad about your life and situation, just think about a person who's more troubled than you, who has gone through more sorrows and problems in life. After thinking about them, just think about the positive things in your life and be grateful for them. This will help you feel good.

some of them are,

- You are breathing oxygen worth lakhs without using machines worth crores.
- You have a heart that is beating all the time.
- You have many secret admirers and prayers for you, who always wish a well-being for you.
- You are not starving.

Maybe these four reasons as enough to be grateful and thankful for life.

We will reach where our destiny will take us. So, be mindful and start your journey to serenity. Destiny will only help us if we help ourselves. Let us put in such efforts, that destiny gets forced to come soon and get us liberated from everything. But, we need to just put effort constantly without expecting the result. Sometimes, results take longer time but having patience is the best option.

XX

The Last Lesson

In the first chapter itself, I had told that if we are on the path and still can't reach the goal then there are three major reasons for it. Two reasons I had told and promised to give the third one in the middle but didn't get a proper chance for it. So here is the third reason. Sometimes we are on the right path but still, we take a lot of time to reach the goal. The reason is that destiny is still far. At such points, we need to have patience and keep on doing our good deeds. Whenever destiny will come, we will reach our path.

Destiny does it all in life. So, there is no need of worrying or stressing about anything. Whatever is written, will happen. No one can stop it from happening. Other than that, no one can take away your fate! It is yours and will remain yours. So don't stress or worry about anything. Whatever happens, it happens for good.

❧

After understanding everything, it is important to apply it in life and retain it. Application work has to be done by you. But I can give you something for maintaining it.

ॐ

12 things you need to think about every day.

1. Nothing in this World is permanent.
2. No one can provide protection or shelter to us. We are completely helpless in certain conditions of life.
3. There is no permanent relation in this universe. Everyone will come and go. You are the only permanent one for you.
4. The soul is always alone and complete within.
5. We are separate from all beings and bodies.
6. Even this body has to be left one day. Everyone's body is just made up of impurities like bones, blood, and muscles. There is nothing to run behind.
7. Everyone in this universe is bound to karmas. No one can escape it until liberated completely from this world.
8. This world will keep on changing always. No one can stop that change. It happens with the time that waits for none.
9. All living beings are like us and we are like them. Let us have a feeling of friendship and compassion towards every living being.
10. Let us be grateful for everyone who has done at least one thing for us in our life.
11. Let's feel mercy towards all the animals and birds being killed or died due to various reasons. Let's feel mercy towards human beings around us who are physically and mentally ill.
12. Let us forgive everyone who has done anything wrong to us. We aren't just forgiving them but we are also making our heart light weighted. It is the most precious organ of the human body. Why unnecessarily fill it with

hardships? Remember, Forgiving can't be done without forgetting

There is only one thing that saves us from this life cycle. He's the god. We have seen above who God is. Also, to clear the third point of the above 12 points.

There are three things from which no one can save us. Let it be our loved ones or the professional ones. No relations can come and save you from death. No relations can save you from your health issues. At the most, they can support you, cry for you or cheer you up. But they can't take away your problems. No relations can save you from increasing age or old age. It will come with time and no one can stop it. Other than that no relative is going to leave a single piece of sweet for you. After you, no one will even leave a single item. That's the kind of love we have in this world. It is an impure form of love. But still, it is necessary for everyone to get confident and to get on the track of spiritualism and happiness.

ಙ

Real Love is something beyond our experience. It is something that has no taking but just giving. It is something that has no sorrow when there's everything from just one side. It is something that has zero expectations and just acceptance of everything. It is something that makes you happy anyhow and in any way. There's no need to do anything for you. This kind of love can usually happen with only God and no others. Once you achieve a certain level of meditation and spiritualism, you will start feeling yourself in everyone. You will start loving everything and everyone. That will be the real kind of love.

There is also another sad reality, I want to talk about. Many times, we make big mistakes in life without realizing them. One such mistake is we give more value to things than humans. For loving, we always chose things over humans. For clearing this concept, let me again give you an example.

Suppose any of your loved persons throw away the most loved thing of yours. What will be your reaction? I am sure you will be angry with that person for your thing. Similarly, in other all places of life, we chose things over people. The live example we can see is, we see everyone more interactive with electronic devices than people. We see everyone valuing their mobiles and gadgets. This behavior might not be similar in other countries. But is a sad truth of India.

Giving more importance to things may make people feel of no importance. Even people need attention and affection to prosper. For that, we need to accept them and help them prosper by giving affection. We need to take care of that, because of us, no one gets a feel of no importance. Let us satisfy everyone too and make this planet an amazing place to live.

୨୦

To wrap up, just telling you about the final stage of meditation, as now I feel you are capable to understand it. It is a stage where we are just a being who is watching everything. We are not the one who is doing everything. We are just the soul, separate from the body. Everything happening is done by my body and not by me. I'm a free soul, full of virtues and good values. When we attain that level in which we feel that we are watching a movie. Nothing is happening to us, it is happening to the body. The day we realize the fact that we are different from our body and the day it comes into action in our everyday life, just understand that you are very near to success.

"Running behind Success for getting Peace, is the biggest foolishness as the Peace is the Success in itself."

ॐ

CONCLUSION

૪૭

I have tried my best for explaining the concepts to you. whatever I have explained is taught by Lord Mahaveer in his various sermons and teachings. Anything written in this book against his teaching might be a human error. This whole work is the result of lords and Gurudev's blessings. I am thankful to all my readers for reaching till here. You all have done a great job. You can also watch the Hindi movie called, 'Ek Cheez Milegi Wonderful' on YouTube, for understanding the concept of senses and happiness in a better way. I just wish you all the best that you come to the path of spiritualism soon and if you are already on it, you achieve the best heights. May God bless you all and all the living beings. Thank You.

-Harsh M. Chheda

૭૩

Lightning Source UK Ltd.
Milton Keynes UK
UKHW010706270223
417728UK00001B/292